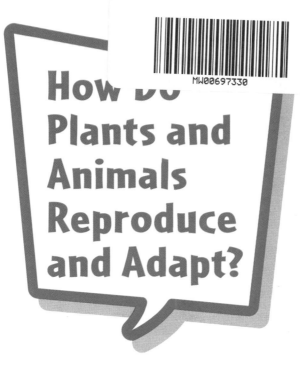

How Do Plants and Animals Reproduce and Adapt?

HOUGHTON MIFFLIN HARCOURT

Printed in Mexico

ISBN: 978-0-544-07322-7

6 7 8 9 10 0908 21 20 19 18 17 16

4500608014   A B C D E F G

Be an Active Reader!

Look at these words.

fertilization   incomplete   physical adaptation
pollination   metamorphosis behavioral adaptation
germination   environment   instinct
complete   adaptation   heredity
    metamorphosis

Look for answers to these questions.

How do plants reproduce?
How do pollen, seeds, and spores travel?
What is the life cycle of a seed plant?
How do animals reproduce?
What is metamorphosis?
Why must a living thing adapt to its environment?
What are physical adaptations?
What are behavioral adaptations?
What is heredity?
What's the difference between instinct and learned behavior?

How do plants reproduce?

Plants grow all over Earth. Cactus plants grow in deserts. Palm trees and orchids grow in rain forests. Mosses grow in swamps. You can even find plants growing in cities. Do you ever wonder how new plants are made?

Plants that make seeds produce new plants through sexual reproduction. Sperm are the male sex cells, and eggs are the female sex cells. Look at the diagram of the flower below. Pollen, found in the anther, contains sperm. Eggs are found in the pistil. Many flowers have anthers and a pistil.

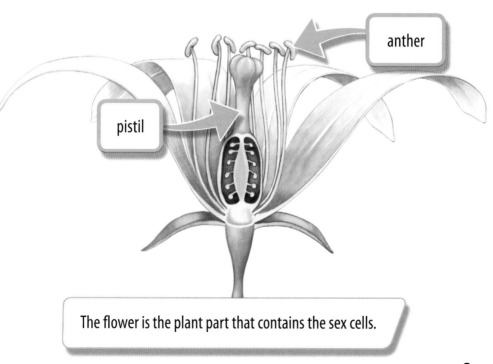

anther

pistil

The flower is the plant part that contains the sex cells.

Moss spores form inside capsules that grow at the ends of stalks.

Fertilization is the joining of an egg and a sperm. When an egg is fertilized, it grows into an embryo inside a seed. The embryo is the first stage of a plant's life.

In most seed plants, the seeds form in flowers. For example, seeds of apple trees form in the apple blossoms. The seeds of other seed plants form in cones. For example, seeds of pine trees form in cones.

Some plants, such as mosses and ferns, don't make seeds. Instead, these plants form spores. A spore is a reproductive structure that can produce new plants. The spores form inside a capsule. The capsule bursts open and releases the spores.

How do pollen, seeds, and spores travel?

Pollination is the transfer of pollen from the anthers to the pistil of a seed plant. How does the pollen get to the pistil? Both wind and water can carry pollen. Animals can also carry pollen. The bee is a good example of a pollinator. A bee goes from flower to flower to drink nectar. Along the way, the bee picks up pollen from anthers and leaves behind pollen on the pistil. That's how flowers are pollinated.

Seeds also travel by wind, water, and animals. Animals transport seeds when they eat fruits and the seeds leave the animals' bodies in their waste. Some seeds have thorns or hooks that attach to an animal's fur and travel on its body.

Like pollen and seeds, spores travel by wind to new places. Many land in places with good light and water. These spores can then grow into new plants.

Wind transports the pollen of grasses and trees.

What is the life cycle of a seed plant?

A seed plant goes through a series of stages in its life. This series is called a life cycle. A seed is planted in soil. Next, the seed sprouts into a tiny plant. Then, the plant grows until it can produce flowers or cones. These are the parts that make more seeds.

Let's use radishes as an example. A radish seed contains the embryo of a radish plant. During the process of germination, the seed sprouts. When the seed sprouts, the embryo in the seed begins to grow into a tiny plant.

As the radish plant grows, it gets larger and grows more roots. When it grows to its full size, it reaches maturity. That's the stage at which an organism can reproduce. Mature plants can make seeds that can grow into new plants.

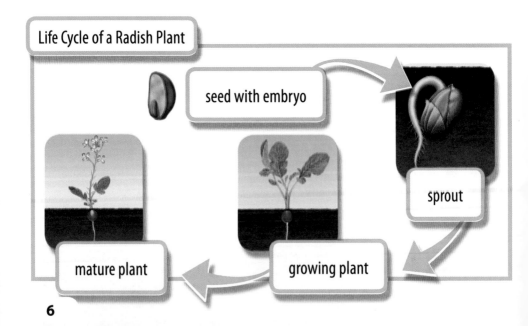

Life Cycle of a Radish Plant

seed with embryo

sprout

mature plant

growing plant

Much of our food comes from plants. You or people you know might grow some of these plants in a garden. Imagine that you want to grow lima beans. What should you do?

First, get a package of lima bean seeds. Next, plant the seeds where they'll get good light. After some time, the seeds will sprout. The plants grow and produce flowers. Then the bean pods appear. Now the plant is mature. The pods contain seeds, which we call beans. They can be planted to grow new lima bean plants.

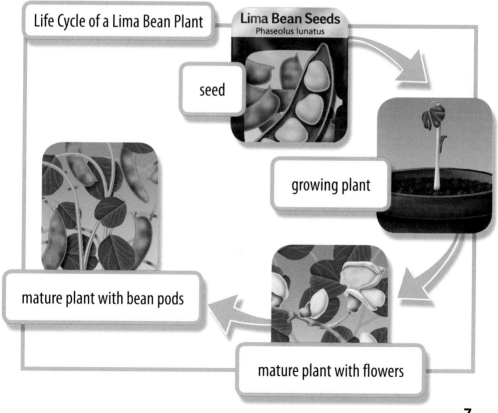

Life Cycle of a Lima Bean Plant

Lima Bean Seeds
Phaseolus lunatus

seed

growing plant

mature plant with bean pods

mature plant with flowers

The temperature of alligator eggs determines whether hatchlings will be male or female.

How do animals reproduce?

Most animals reproduce sexually. A sperm from a male joins with an egg from a female. The fertilized egg can grow into a new animal.

The eggs of some animals, such as the frog, are fertilized outside the female's body. Eggs of other animals, such as the alligator, are fertilized inside the female's body. The female alligator digs a hollow in a nest of leaves and grass. She then lays her eggs. She covers the eggs with more leaves and grass and watches over the nest.

After about two months, the young alligators begin to squeak. That's the sign that they are ready to hatch. After they hatch, the female alligator carries the hatchlings to the water. She carries them in her mouth. When alligators are about 10 years old, they can mate and produce young.

Other animals, such as lions and cows, don't lay eggs. The female gives birth to live young. She cares for the young and feeds them milk.

Female horses give birth to live young. They care for their young and feed them milk.

What is metamorphosis?

Some animals have young that look very different from the adult animals. These animals go through the process of complete metamorphosis. In complete metamorphosis, animals go through four stages in their life cycle. Animals that go through complete metamorphosis include beetles and butterflies. In a butterfly's first stage, an egg hatches into a larva. The larva is also known as a caterpillar. At this stage, the young is very different from the adult. Next, the caterpillar develops into a pupa inside a chrysalis. While in the chrysalis, the pupa also becomes an adult butterfly. Finally, the butterfly splits the chrysalis and flies out.

egg

Butterflies go through complete metamorphosis.

adult butterfly

larva

pupa

Some insects, such as the dragonfly, go through incomplete metamorphosis. In incomplete metamorphosis, there are three stages of development.

A dragonfly hatches from its egg as a nymph. A nymph is an immature form. The nymph resembles an adult dragonfly except that the nymph doesn't have wings. The nymph grows larger and molts, or sheds its outer covering. It molts several times and grows wings. The dragonfly has reached the adult stage.

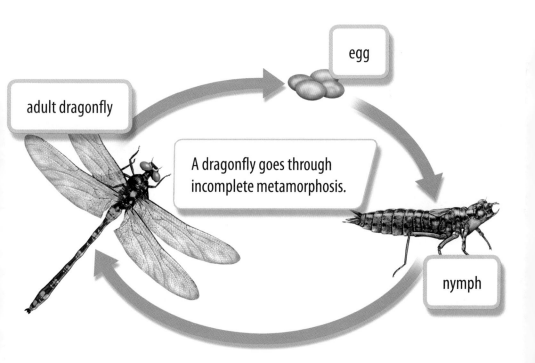

egg

adult dragonfly

A dragonfly goes through incomplete metamorphosis.

nymph

Why must a living thing adapt to its environment?

Deserts, rain forests, and oceans are environments. An environment is all the living and nonliving things that surround and affect an organism. The picture below shows a wetland environment. The environment includes all of the plants, animals, water, air, and land around any living thing in the wetland.

Plants need air, water, and food. Animals need all of these things as well as shelter. Living things depend on their environment to provide the things they need.

Birds and other animals find air, food, water, and a safe place to live in this wetland environment.

Environments on Earth have different features. For example, deserts have little rainfall. Rain forests are hot and humid and have a large amount of rainfall. Each living thing must be able to survive in its environment.

Plants and animals have adaptations that allow them to live in their environment. An adaptation is a trait or characteristic that helps an organism survive in its environment. For example, the saguaro cactus has a large root system that spreads far from its trunk. The root system helps the plant collect water when it rains.

Adaptations help the saguaro cactus survive in places with little water.

water lily

Adaptations help the water lily survive in water.

What are physical adaptations?

A physical adaptation is an adaptation in a body part. For example, a macaw is a parrot that is adapted to life in the rain forest. The macaw has a large, powerful beak. This feature helps it break open nuts and seeds from rain forest trees. The macaw also has feet that help it grip tree branches and hold objects.

A mallard is a type of duck that is adapted for life in a wetland environment. The mallard has a bill that helps it catch food underwater. Its webbed feet help it move quickly both on and under water.

The macaw's beak is an adaptation to rain forest life.

A mallard's bill is an adaptation to wetland life.

Polar bears are adapted to the freezing environment of the Arctic. The polar bear has a long snout. The snout helps it poke into holes in the ice to pull out its favorite meal—a seal. Polar bears also have wide feet with claws. These foot adaptations help them walk on the ice without slipping.

Camels are adapted for life in a desert environment. There, most plants are tough and prickly. The camel has sharp teeth that help it eat these plants. Camels also have wide feet that help them walk on sand without sinking.

Look at the photograph of the desert. What other physical adaptations do you think a camel might have?

What are behavioral adaptations?

A behavioral adaptation is a way of acting that helps an animal survive. Have you seen a movie or television show about emperor penguins? If so, you probably saw how the males huddle together to stay warm. This is an example of a behavioral adaptation.

An instinct is an example of a behavioral adaptation. An instinct is a behavior an animal knows how to do without having to learn it. For example, many Arctic animals dig dens in the snow to live in during the coldest winter months. Some desert animals dig dens in the sand, where they spend the hottest part of the day.

Sea turtles hatch on land. By instinct, the hatchlings use light to figure out the direction of the ocean.

Arctic terns fly back and forth from the Northern to the Southern Hemisphere. This is a behavioral adaptation.

Bears have many behavioral adaptations that help them survive winter. From late summer to fall, bears eat up to five times as much as they usually do each day. By the end of fall, they have added a layer of fat to their body. Then they look for a place to spend the winter. It might be a hollow in a tree or a hole under a pile of leaves and branches. The bears spend the winter in this den. They don't come out to eat or drink. They live on their layer of fat.

Humpback whales leave Alaska in the fall. They swim to the warm ocean waters near Hawaii to spend the winter and give birth to their young. Then, in spring, they head back to the Alaskan coast, where they find food.

What is heredity?

Heredity is the passing of traits from parents to their offspring. Heredity happens in all living things. Plants inherit traits such as flower color. Flower color is passed from adult plants to their offspring.

Animals inherit traits, too. That is why animal family members resemble each other. One example of an inherited trait is the stripes on a tiger.

Skunks have inherited traits. One is fur color. Another is their ability to spray.

Every living thing has genes. Genes are the chemical instructions that control traits. In organisms that reproduce sexually, half of a living thing's traits come from the mother, and half come from the father. Genes are found inside sex cells. When male and female sex cells join, the new cell has genes from the parents' cells.

Living things also have traits that are caused by the environment. That means that the environment can change living things. For example, tadpoles, or frog larvae, swim in ponds. If a pond dries up, the tadpoles living there go through metamorphosis faster than usual. They become adult frogs faster than tadpoles living in a pond full of water.

Air temperature can also cause changes to living things. You learned that the temperature of alligator eggs determines whether baby alligators will be male or female. If the temperature is 86 °Fahrenheit (°F) or less, the young will be female. If it's 93 °F or greater, the young will be male. If the temperature is between 86 °F and 93 °F, there will be a mix of male and female young.

Light can cause changes to living things. These sunflowers will grow toward the source of light.

What's the difference between instinct and learned behavior?

Animals are able to learn some different behaviors. A learned behavior is a behavior that an animal develops as a result of experience or by observing other animals.

Remember that instincts are behaviors that animals are born with. They help animals live and stay safe, but they are not learned. Rattlesnakes know by instinct to get away from danger. If they do get cornered, they may rattle their tail. This is a warning to stay away!

The American White Pelican has an especially large bill. The bird knows by instinct how to catch fish with it.

Each fall, monarch butterflies fly south. They go from the United States to Mexico, where it is warm. In the spring, they fly back. They do this instinctively. Many types of birds also know by instinct when it is time to migrate to a warmer place.

A mother bottlenose dolphin whistles to her young. The calf learns to recognize its mother. This is a learned bahavior.

When a goose hatches, the parent is the first organism it sees. Wherever the parent goes, the young goose will follow. This behavior is an example of instinct. The young goose watches the parent and learns how to get food. This is an example of a learned behavior.

Animals can learn more difficult behaviors. Young coyotes learn to hunt from older animals. They also learn how to behave as part of a pack. Young prairie dogs watch adults to learn how to protect themselves. They learn to recognize the warning call. When they hear it, they dive into their burrow for safety.

Model Environmental Change

Gather these materials: shoebox with lid, cardboard, scissors, tape, and a small potted plant. Cut a large hole in one end of the shoebox. Cut two pieces of cardboard, each the same height and half the width of the box. Tape one piece of cardboard to the inside of the shoebox at one-third of its length. Tape the other piece on the opposite side at two-thirds of the length. Stand the box so that the hole is at the top. Place the watered plant inside the box. Tape the lid on. Wait for 5 days and then open the box. You'll see how light affects the direction of a plant's growth.

Write an Article

Write an article for a website about animal behavior and adaptation. First, choose an animal. Use the Internet and other resources to learn about the animal. Find out which behaviors of the animal are instinctive and which are learned. Find out how the animal has adapted to its environment. Then write your article.

Glossary

adaptation [ad·uhp·TAY·shuhn] A trait or characteristic that helps an organism survive.

behavioral adaptation [bih·HAYV·yu·ruhl ad·uhp·TAY·shuhn] Something an animal does that helps it survive.

complete metamorphosis [kuhm·PLEET met·uh·MAWR·fuh·sis] A complex change that most insects undergo that includes larva and pupa stages.

environment [en·VY·ruhn·muhnt] All the living and nonliving things that surround and affect an organism.

fertilization [fer·tl·li·ZAY·shuhn] The joining together of a sperm and an egg cell.

germination [jer·muh·NAY·shuhn] The sprouting of a seed.

heredity [huh·RED·ih·tee] The process by which traits are passed from parents to offspring.

incomplete metamorphosis [in·kuhm·PLEET met·uh·MAWR·fuh·sis] Developmental change in some insects in which a nymph hatches from an egg and gradually develops into an adult.

instinct [IN·stinkt] A behavior an animal knows how to do without having to learn it.

physical adaptation [FIZ·ih·kuhl ad·uhp·TAY·shuhn] An adaptation to a body part.

pollination [pol·uh·NAY·shuhn] The transfer of pollen from a male plant part to a female plant part of seed plants.